Cambridge Discovery Readers

Level 2

Series editor: Nicholas Tims

Parties and Presents: Three short stories

by Katherine Mansfield

Retold by Margaret Johnson

CAMBRIDGE UNIVERSITY PRESS
Cambridge, New York, Melbourne, Madrid, Cape Town,
Singapore, São Paulo, Delhi, Mexico City

Cambridge University Press
79 Anson Road, #06-04/06, Singapore 079906

www.cambridge.org

This American English edition is based on *Parties and Presents: Three short stories*,
ISBN 978-84-8323-836-3 first published by Cambridge University Press in 2010.

First published 2010
American English edition 2011
Reprinted 2012

Printed in Singapore by Tien Wah Press

ISBN 978-0-521-18159-4 Paperback American English edition

Illustrations by Jo Blake (Beehive Illustration)

Exercises by hyphen

The publishers are grateful to the following for permission to reproduce
photographic material:

© Alberto Ruggieri | Illustration Works | Corbis for cover image

Music composed by Boccherini and published by Shockwave-Sound.com

Contents

BEFORE YOU READ

1 Look at the pictures in the book.

1 Who are the main people in the first story?

....

2 Where do the people go in the second story?

....

3 What do the people play with in the third story?

....

The Garden Party

It was a lovely day for a garden party. The weather was warm, with no wind, and the sky was blue. The garden was ready for the party. The grass was short and very green in the sun. There were hundreds and hundreds of beautiful roses everywhere.

The workmen arrived to put up the marquee[1] while the family were still eating breakfast.

"Where do you want the marquee to go, Mother?" asked Meg.

"My dear child, don't ask me," answered Mrs. Sheridan, her mother. "I'm leaving everything to you children this year."

But Meg's hair was wet, and Jose was still wearing her nightclothes, so they couldn't go out to speak to the men.

"You go, Laura," Meg said. "You're the artist in the family. You know about these things."

Laura ran outside, still holding the piece of bread she was eating. She felt very happy. She liked deciding things.

Four men stood waiting in the garden. They looked strong.

"Why did I bring my bread out with me?" thought Laura, feeling stupid. But there was nowhere to put it, and she couldn't throw it away.

"Good morning," she said importantly to the men.

"Oh, dear," she thought. "I sound just like Mother." Her face went red. Now she felt like a little girl.

"Oh . . . uh . . . have you come about the marquee?" she said.

"That's right, Miss," said one of the men. He was tall and thin, and he smiled at her. "That's it."

His smile was so friendly that Laura felt better. What nice eyes he had – small, but such a dark blue! She looked at the others, and they were smiling, too. "Don't worry – we're very nice," Laura thought their smiles were saying to her, and she smiled back. How very nice workmen were! And what a beautiful day! But she mustn't talk about the day. She had to talk to them about the marquee.

"Well," she said, "what about putting it on the grass over there?"

The men turned and looked.

"No, I don't think that's the right place," said the tall man.

He turned back to Laura. "You see, with a marquee, you want it to be somewhere you can really see it. What about over there, in front of those trees?"

In front of the karaka trees! Oh dear, they were so lovely

in the sunlight, with their large leaves and yellow fruit. Did the marquee really have to go there?

But three of the men were already walking over there with the marquee. Only the tall man stayed behind. He was smelling some flowers.

Laura forgot all about the karaka trees as she watched him.

"That's wonderful!" she thought. "He likes the smell of flowers! I don't know any other men like that. Oh, workmen are nice. Why can't I have workmen for friends? The boys who come to dinner on Sunday nights aren't interested in smelling flowers!"

The tall man was drawing something on a piece of paper. Laura watched him. People like her weren't friends with workmen. It was because of class[2]. Some people thought they were better than others, because of their name or because they were rich. Well, she didn't feel like that!

Over by the karaka trees, the other men were busy putting the marquee up. They called to each other in a friendly way. Laura loved it. And to show how happy she was, to show the tall man she was like them, she ate some of her bread as she looked at his little picture. She felt just like a worker.

"Laura, Laura, where are you? Telephone, Laura!" a voice called from the house.

"Coming!" she answered, and then she ran quickly across the grass and up to the house.

Inside, she found her father and her brother Laurie getting ready to go to work.

"Laura," said Laurie, "if you have time, can you take a look at my jacket before this afternoon? Can you see if it looks all right?"

"Yes, of course," agreed Laura, and then she felt so happy she ran to Laurie and put her arms around him.

"Oh, I do love parties," she said. "Don't you?"

"Oh, yes," answered Laurie in a warm voice, then he

pushed her softly away. "Don't forget your telephone call," he said.

Her telephone call! Of course. "Hello?" she said into the phone. "Kitty? Oh, hello, good morning, dear. Of course you can come to lunch, dear, but I don't think it will be anything very special. Yes, isn't it a beautiful morning? What's that? You're going to wear your white dress? Oh, yes."

Then Laura heard her mother – she was calling from upstairs. "Just a minute," she said to Kitty, "Mother's saying something."

Laura sat back. "What, Mother?" she shouted. "I can't hear you."

"Kitty can wear the lovely hat that she wore on Sunday," Mrs. Sheridan called.

"Mother wants you to wear that lovely hat you wore on Sunday," Laura said into the phone. "Good. See you at one o'clock then. Bye."

Laura put the phone down. Then she stood, listening. All the doors in the house were open. The house was full of the sound of people moving and talking. She could feel a soft wind traveling everywhere. The sun was dancing through the open windows. It was all so beautiful! The front doorbell rang.

Laura heard their servant Sadie going to answer it. Then she heard a man talking.

"I'm sure I don't know," Sadie said. "Wait. I'll ask Mrs. Sheridan."

Laura went into the hall[3]. "What is it, Sadie?" she asked.

"This man's brought some flowers, Miss Laura," Sadie told her.

Laura looked and saw lots and *lots* of pink lily flowers

by the door. "But there are so many!" Laura said. "It has to be a mistake! Sadie, go and find my mother."

But at that moment, Mrs. Sheridan came down the stairs. "It's all right," she said. "I asked for all these."

She put her hand on Laura's arm. "I was walking past the flower shop yesterday, and I saw these lilies in the window. And I thought, 'For once in my life, I must have enough lilies. I must have them for the garden party.'"

Laura put her arm around her mother. "I thought you were leaving the party to us," she said.

"Darling, it's only a few flowers," her mother replied. "I fell in love with them."

The man brought more lilies. "Put them on both sides of the door, please," Mrs. Sheridan told him. "What do you think, Laura? Do they look nice there?"

"I think they look lovely, Mother," Laura said.

Jose and Meg were in the living room with Hans.

"I think we'll move all the furniture out except for the piano and the chairs," Jose was saying.

"Good idea," agreed Meg.

"Hans, move these tables out and clean this carpet[4], please," said Jose. "Oh, and can you ask Mother and Miss Laura to come here?"

"Yes, Miss Jose."

Jose turned to Meg. "I want to sing this afternoon. Let's try some songs. What about 'This Life Is Weary[5]'?"

Jose began to play the piano.

"This Life Is Weary" was a sad song. As she began to sing, Jose made her face very sad. Mrs. Sheridan and Laura came into the room and stood to listen.

When the song finished, Jose stopped being sad and

smiled a big smile. "Do I sound all right, Mother?" she asked.

But before Mrs. Sheridan could answer, Sadie came into the room.

"What is it, Sadie?" Mrs. Sheridan asked.

"Excuse me, Madam. Cook needs the names for the sandwiches." At parties, they always wrote names for the different plates of sandwiches. People wanted to know what was in them.

When Laura looked at her mother's face, she thought, "Mother has forgotten to write the names."

"Tell Cook that she'll have them in 10 minutes," Mrs. Sheridan told Sadie.

"Yes, Mrs. Sheridan," replied Sadie, and she left.

"Now, Laura," said Mrs. Sheridan. "Come and help me to write out the names. Meg, go and dry your hair. Jose, go and finish getting dressed. And be nice to Cook if you go into the kitchen. She's very busy today. You know she can get angry when she's busy. I must say, I feel a little afraid of her this morning! Come on, Laura."

Laura and her mother wrote out the names of the sandwiches on pretty pieces of paper, and then Laura took them down to the kitchen. Jose was in there, being nice to Cook.

"Look at all this wonderful food!" she was saying. "How many different sandwiches are there, Cook?"

"Fifteen, Miss Jose," answered Cook.

"Lovely!" Jose said.

Cook was cleaning some bits of bread off the table. She gave Jose a big smile.

"Godber's has come with the cakes," Sadie said, looking out of the window.

"Well, bring them in and put them on the table, my girl," Cook told her.

Sadie went out to the door. After a moment she came back with the cakes and put them down on the table. Then she went back out to talk to the man from Godber's.

Laura and Jose looked at the cakes. They were too old to care about such things, of course, but the cakes certainly looked very nice.

"The cakes make me remember our birthday parties when we were children," Laura told her sister.

"Do they?" said Jose, who didn't like to think about the past.

"Have one each, my dears," Cook said. "Your mother won't know."

So soon after breakfast! What an idea! But the girls didn't like to say no to Cook, and two minutes later they were full of cake.

"Let's go into the garden, out by the back door," Laura said to Jose. "I want to see how the men are getting along with the marquee. They're really nice men."

But they couldn't get out of the back door. Cook, Sadie, Hans, and the man from Godber's were standing there.

"Oh!" Cook was saying. She sounded sad.

Sadie had a hand on her cheek. Laura thought both she and Hans were worried about something. They were listening to the man from Godber's.

"What is it?" asked Laura, looking at their faces.

"A man is dead," Cook told her.

"Dead?" said Laura. "Where? How? When?" She wanted to know everything.

Cook started to speak, but Godber's man wasn't going to let anyone else tell the story.

"Do you know those little cottages[6] just below here, Miss?" he asked.

"Yes, of course," replied Laura.

"Well, there's a young man who lives there. Scott's his name. He fell from his horse this morning. He hit his head on the road. He's dead."

"Dead!" Laura said again, looking at him.

"Yes, Miss," agreed Godber's man. "They were taking the body home as I came up here." And then he said to Cook, "He had a wife and five little ones, you know."

"It's terrible," said Cook. "Terrible."

"Jose, come here," Laura said quietly, holding her sister's arm and pulling her out of the kitchen.

"Jose," she said, after the door closed. "How are we going to stop everything?"

Jose just looked at her. She didn't understand. "Stop everything?" she asked. "What do you mean?"

"Stop the garden party, of course!" said Laura.

"Stop the garden party? My dear Laura, don't be silly[7]!"

Laura looked at her sister. Why didn't she understand? "We can't have a garden party with a dead man just outside the front gate[8]!" she said.

It wasn't quite true to say the dead man was just outside the front gate. The cottages were on a road at the bottom of a big hill from the house. But they were close. Mrs. Sheridan often said they were *too* close. The cottages were small, dark houses on a smelly road. Working people lived in them, and there were children everywhere. When they were young, Mrs. Sheridan didn't let her children go there. Now that they were older, Laura and Laurie sometimes walked past the houses, but they didn't really like to.

"This poor man is dead!" Laura said. "We can't just drink tea and play music with that poor woman just down the road!"

"Oh, Laura!" Jose said. She was starting to get really angry now. "We can't stop playing music every time someone

gets hurt! I'm really sorry this man is dead, but we can't do anything about it."

"I'm going to talk to Mother," said Laura, walking away.

"Go on then!" said Jose, still angry.

Mrs. Sheridan was in her room, trying on a hat.

"What is it, Laura?" she asked when she saw her daughter's face. "You're so white."

"A man's died, Mother," Laura told her.

Mrs. Sheridan looked worried. "Not in the garden?" she asked.

"No, no!"

Mrs. Sheridan smiled. "Oh, thank goodness for that!" she said, and went back to her hat.

"But listen, Mother," said Laura, and she told her the story. "So of course we can't have our party, can we?" she said. "The family lives really near to us. They're almost our neighbors."

"But darling," Mrs. Sheridan said. "We only know about it because the man from Godber's told us. Of course we can still have our party."

Laura sat down. She didn't understand how everyone could feel so differently from her. "But, Mother, isn't it very unkind of us?"

Mrs. Sheridan didn't answer. She got up and came over to her daughter, carrying the hat. She put it on Laura's head. "My child!" she said. "The hat is yours. It's much too young for me. You look beautiful! Take a look in the mirror."

But Laura didn't want to. "But, Mother," she started, but Mrs. Sheridan spoke angrily.

"You're being very silly, Laura," she told her daughter coldly.

“I don’t understand,” said Laura again, and she walked quickly to her bedroom. There she saw herself in the mirror: a pretty girl with a lovely black and gold hat.

“Is that really me?” she thought. She looked and looked. And then she thought, “Is Mother right?” And now she

hoped her mother *was* right because she wanted to wear the hat to the party.

"Am I being silly?" she thought.

Just for a moment, Laura thought about the poor woman and her children again. In her head, she saw the man's friends carrying his body back to his house. But now it wasn't quite real. It was more like a picture in the newspaper.

"I can think about it after the party is over," she decided. And that was a good idea.

Lunch was over by half past one. By half past two, they were all ready for the party. Laurie arrived back from work. When she saw him, Laura remembered about the man and his family again. She wanted to tell him about it.

"Maybe Laurie agrees with the others. Then I won't worry about it anymore," she thought. "Then I'll forget it."

"Laurie!" she called.

"Hello!" He was halfway upstairs, but he turned to look at her. "Laura!" he said. "You look wonderful! What a lovely hat!"

Laura smiled up at him. "Is it?" she asked, and then somehow she forgot to tell him about the dead man after that.

Soon everyone started to arrive for the party. The music started. Waiters[9] ran from the house to the marquee. People were everywhere, walking, smiling, and smelling the flowers. Laura thought they were like beautiful birds visiting her family's garden for the afternoon. How wonderful it was to be with people who were so happy! How nice it was to kiss cheeks and smile into eyes! And everyone was so nice to her.

"Darling Laura, how well you look!" someone told her.

"Laura, what a beautiful hat!" someone else said.

"Laura, you look almost Spanish! I've never seen you look so lovely!"

And Laura felt very warm inside. She felt *so* happy. She smiled and smiled and asked softly, "Do you want some tea? Won't you have an ice? The fruit ices are very special."

Laura looked after everybody. She wanted everyone to have a nice time – the musicians, too. She ran to her father and asked him, "Daddy darling, can the musicians have something to drink? It's very hot."

And slowly, slowly, the beautiful afternoon passed like a flower closing up as night falls.

"We've never been to a more lovely garden party," people said as they were leaving. "Thank you so much."

Laura helped her mother with the good-byes. They stood side by side until everyone left.

"All over," said Mrs. Sheridan. "Thank goodness. Go and find the others, Laura. We'll have some coffee. I'm so tired. Why do you children always ask me to have these parties?"

And they all sat down in the empty marquee.

"Have a sandwich, Daddy dear," said Laura.

"Thanks." Mr. Sheridan ate the sandwich quietly. Then he said, "Did you hear about the man who died?"

Mrs. Sheridan held up her hand. "Yes, we did, my dear," she said. "Laura wanted to stop the party! Can you believe it?"

Laura didn't want to remember it. She just wanted to sit and think about the party. "Oh, Mother!" she said. "Let's not talk about that now."

"But it was very bad," Mr. Sheridan said. "The man was married, you know. He lived just down the road in the cottages. His wife has six children, they say."

Nobody spoke for a moment. Mrs. Sheridan looked down at her cup. Then she looked up. There was still a lot of food on the table. She had one of her ideas.

"I know," she said. "We can send that poor woman some of this food. There will be lots of people. And the children will be hungry, too."

She stood up. "Come on, Laura, help me put it into a basket."

Laura stood up, too, but her face was worried. "But Mother, do you really think it's a good idea?" she asked. Again, she felt different from everybody. To take the food from their party to that woman! It was wrong!

"Of course it's a good idea!" answered Mrs. Sheridan angrily. "What's wrong with you today, Laura? An hour or two ago you didn't want to stop talking about it and now . . ."

Laura didn't want her mother to be angry with her again. "All right!" she said. "I'll get a basket." She brought a basket from the house, and her mother put lots of food into it.

"I'll ask Sadie to take it," Laura said.

"No," her mother answered. "Take it yourself, darling."

Laura looked down at her party clothes.

"No," said Mrs. Sheridan, "you don't need to change your clothes. Run down there like that."

"All right, Mother," said Laura and she turned to go.

"Wait," Mrs. Sheridan stopped her. "Take the lilies, too. Poor people like that never see flowers like those."

"All those pink flowers, too!" thought Laura, looking at them. "Oh, no!"

"The color from the lilies will get on Laura's dress," said Jose.

She was right. Good old Jose. Just in time.

"Yes, all right. Just the basket then," agreed Mrs. Sheridan. And she gave Laura the basket of food.

The sun was starting to go down as Laura left the house. After the noise of the afternoon, everything was very quiet. Nothing felt real to Laura. It was difficult to believe she was really going down the hill to the dead man's cottage. She didn't want to think about it, so she thought about the party. It wasn't difficult because all the sounds and smells from the afternoon were still with her. She could hear voices and laughing and spoons on cups. She could smell the smell of the grass and the roses. It was all still so real to her that soon there was no room inside her for anything else but the party. How strange. She looked up at the sky, and all she thought was, "Yes, it was a very good party."

She was almost at the cottages now. Children played outside their front doors. Men talked. Women walked quickly by. Lights were on in some of the windows. Laura walked quickly. All the sounds and smells of the lovely afternoon left her head. She thought about her hat and her white dress. "Why didn't I change?" she thought. "Are people looking at me? Why am I here? This is wrong – wrong!"

"I'll go back," she thought, but it was too late. This was the house. There were lots of people standing outside. It was

too dark now to see their faces. As Laura came near, they stopped talking.

"Is . . . is this Mrs. Scott's house?" she asked. She felt afraid and knew it probably showed in her voice.

"It is," said a woman, and Laura walked up to the house and knocked on the door. Oh, she really wanted to be away from those people looking at her!

"I'll just leave the basket and go," she thought.

The door opened. A little woman in black looked at her.

"Are you Mrs. Scott?" asked Laura.

But the woman answered, "Walk in please, Miss."

"No!" said Laura. "I don't want to come in. I only want to leave this basket. Mother sent –"

But the little woman just said again, "Come in, Miss."

Laura walked into a kitchen. There was a woman sitting by the fire.

"Em," said the little woman. "Em! It's a young lady to see you." She looked at Laura. "I'm her sister, Miss," she told Laura. "I'm afraid Em doesn't really want to talk to anyone just now."

"Of course not," said Laura, who wanted to run out of the door. "Please, I only want to leave this basket . . ." she said, but at that moment the woman at the fire turned to look at her. Her eyes and her face were red from crying.

Laura knew what she was thinking. She didn't understand why Laura was there in her house. She didn't want Laura in her house in her white dress and silly hat. As Laura watched, the woman began to cry again.

"All right, Em," said the little woman. "I'll thank the lady."

"You understand, Miss, I'm sure," she said, and Laura saw that her eyes were red, too.

Laura only wanted to get out, to get away. A door opened, and she walked, but it wasn't the door to the outside. It was the door to a bedroom. Laura looked and saw the dead man on the bed.

"Take a look at him, Miss," said the little woman. "Don't be afraid."

The little woman pulled the sheet from the dead man's face.

"There's nothing bad to see," she told Laura. "He looks all right. Come on, Miss."

Laura came.

She looked at the man. He was young, and he looked asleep. But he wasn't going to wake up again. His eyes weren't ever going to open. He was never going to see again. Garden parties and baskets and pretty dresses and hats were nothing to him. He was far from all those things. The little woman was right – there was nothing bad to see. He was wonderful. Beautiful. And it was so sad.

Laura began to cry. She didn't know what to say.

"I'm sorry about my hat," she said, and this time she didn't wait for the little woman to open the door. She ran out of the house, past all those people standing outside the house in the dark, and up the road. Home – she just wanted to get home. She *had* to get home.

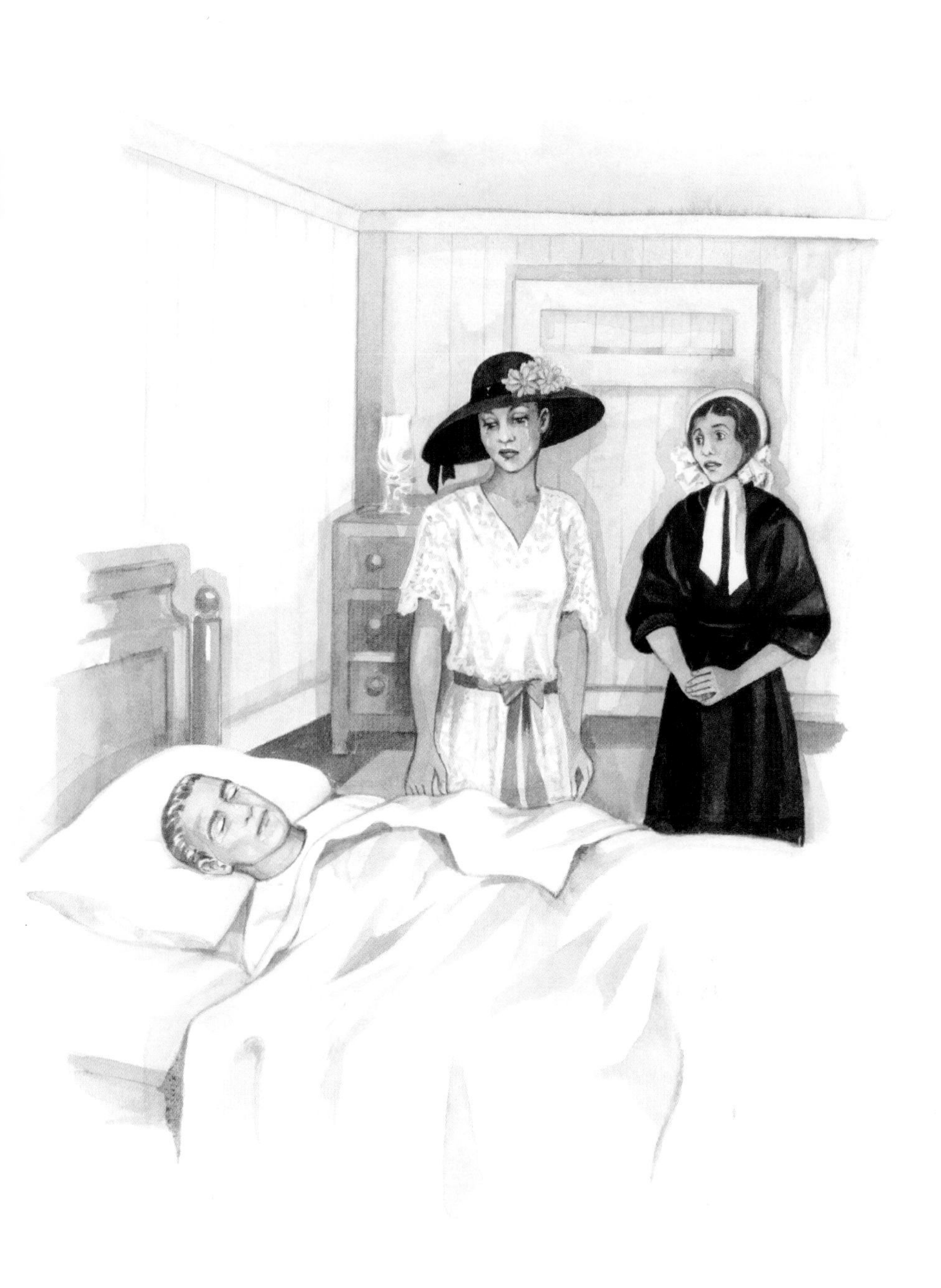

At the corner, she met Laurie. She was very happy to see him.

"Is that you, Laura?" he asked.

"Yes."

"Mother was worried. Was it all right?"

"Yes," she said. "Oh, Laurie!" Laura took his arm and stood close to him.

"You aren't crying, are you?" asked her brother.

"No," said Laura, but she was.

Laurie put his arm around her. "Don't cry," he said in a warm and loving voice. "Was it really bad?"

"No," Laura cried. "But, Laurie . . ."

She stopped and looked at her brother. "Isn't life . . . isn't life . . ." but she didn't know how to say what she wanted to say.

But Laurie understood. "Isn't it?" he agreed.

ACTIVITIES PAGES 4–12

1 **Put the sentences in order.**

1 Mrs. Sheridan wants Kitty to wear her lovely hat. ☐
2 Mrs. Sheridan, Laura, and Meg listen to Jose singing and playing the piano. ☐
3 Laura tells Laurie that she loves parties. ☐
4 Jose says that she wants to sing at the garden party. ☐
5 Laura forgets about her telephone call. ☐
6 The workmen arrive to put up the marquee. [1]
7 A man brings many pink lily flowers to the house. ☐
8 One of the workmen smells the flowers. ☐
9 Laura watches the workmen and feels happy. ☐
10 Laura goes out to speak to the workmen. ☐

2 **Underline the correct words in each sentence.**

1 There are hundreds and hundreds of *karaka trees* / *roses* in the garden.
2 *Mrs. Sheridan* / *Meg* asks Laura to go out and speak to the workmen.
3 The tall man says to put the marquee *in front of the karaka trees* / *on the grass*.
4 Laura thinks that the workmen *are nice* / *don't like smelling flowers*.
5 Sadie asks *Laura* / *Mrs. Sheridan* about the lilies.
6 Mrs. Sheridan wants to have lots of lilies for the *garden party* / *living room*.
7 Jose sings a *sad* / *happy* song.

ACTIVITIES PAGES 13–20

3 Are the sentences true (*T*) or false (*F*)?

1 The Sheridan girls write out the names for the sandwiches. [F]
2 Laura learns from Cook that a young man is dead. [ ]
3 Jose doesn't want to stop the garden party. [ ]
4 The dead man's family lives far from the Sheridans. [ ]
5 The Sheridan girls went to the cottages when they were children. [ ]
6 Laura decides to think about the dead man after the garden party. [ ]
7 Laura enjoys herself at the garden party. [ ]

4 Who or what do the underlined words refer to in these lines from the text?

1 I must say, I feel a little afraid of her this morning! (page 13)
Cook
2 "Have one each, my dears," (page 13) ....
3 They were listening to the man from Godber's. (page 15)
....
4 Why didn't she understand? (page 15) ....
5 She was starting to get really angry now. (page 16)
....
6 She wanted to tell him about it. (page 19) ....
7 "Is it?" (page 19) ....
8 Laura thought they were like beautiful birds visiting her family's garden for the afternoon. (page 19)
....

ACTIVITIES PAGES 21–28

5 Complete the sentences with the names in the box.

Laura (x3)	Laurie	Mrs. Scott's sister
Mrs. Scott	Mrs. Sheridan	Mr. Sheridan

1 ....Laura.... and Mrs. Sheridan say good-bye to all their guests as they leave.
2 .... is tired after the party.
3 .... is sad for the dead man's family.
4 .... takes the party food to the dead man's wife.
5 .... invites Laura into the cottage.
6 .... doesn't want to talk to Laura.
7 .... feels afraid at the cottage.
8 Laura meets .... on the way home from the cottage.

6 Answer the questions.

1 Why does Laura think about the party again when she's going to the cottage?

....

2 Why does Laura think the people outside the cottage are looking at her?

....

3 What does Laura do when she sees the dead man's body?

....

4 How does Laurie show he understands how Laura feels?

....

Her First Ball

Leila was in a taxi with the Sheridan girls, Meg, Jose, and Laura, and their brother Laurie. They were on their way to a ball. Leila was very excited about the evening. "Who will I meet?" she thought. "Who will I dance with?"

As the taxi passed by the dancing lights of all the houses, Leila's arm was on the arm of the seat. To Leila, it almost felt like the arm of a young man – of a dance partner.

"You say you haven't been to a ball before, Leila?" cried one of the Sheridan girls. "I can't believe it!"

"We live in the country," Leila replied softly. "It's miles to the nearest town." She really was *so* excited, but she tried not to show it because the others weren't very excited. They were always going to balls. But for Leila, *everything* was new. Everything made her feel excited . . . Meg's flowers, Jose's dress, Laura's little dark head, pushing above her white coat like a flower in the snow.

Her cousin Laurie took some new gloves[10] from some soft paper and threw the paper away. Oh, that paper! Leila wanted to keep it. She wanted to remember everything about this night for the rest of her life!

Laurie put his hand on his sister Laura's knee. "I can have the third and ninth dances, can't I, Twig?" he said.

"Oh, how wonderful to have a brother!" Leila thought. She was an only child. No one had a special name like Twig for her.

"I've never seen your hair look so lovely, Jose," Meg said to her sister, and Leila almost wanted to cry. They were so nice to each other!

But there was no time for crying. Here they were, arriving at the ball already! The road was full of moving lights and people.

"Hold on to me, Leila," said Laura. "So you don't get lost."

Leila held onto Laura's soft, white coat, and they hurried inside, pushing past everyone and into the ladies' room.

The little room was full of girls talking – the noise was very loud. Everyone was taking their coats off and putting them down onto two long seats. Then they all wanted to look in the little mirror. Dark girls, blond girls were looking at their hair and their dresses. And because they were all laughing, Leila thought they were all lovely.

"Help me with my hair, darling," cried someone.

"My dress!" cried another. "It's dirty at the bottom!"

Then someone called, "Pass them along, pass them along!" And a little basket of dance programs went around the room. The thin books were *beautiful*! They were pink and silver[11] with pink pencils.

Leila took one from the basket. She opened it excitedly. But there wasn't time to read the names of all the dances. Meg was calling, "Ready, Leila?"

"Yes," answered Leila, and they pushed through all the people to get to the ballroom.

It was very loud in the ballroom, too. "How will we hear the music when we're dancing?" Leila thought. She was so happy to be there. She wasn't afraid anymore.

Leila smiled, thinking for a moment of only a few hours ago. "I was so afraid, I wanted to ask Mother to phone the Sheridans to say I couldn't come to the ball!" she remembered to herself. "I was thinking about home. I wanted to be back home so badly, back in the quiet country. I wanted to hear the baby owls[12] crying out in the night. But now! Oh, I'm so happy I'm here!" And she looked around the room again with a big smile on her face.

All the girls were on one side of the room, and all the men were on the other. Their parents were at the end of the room, watching everything.

"This is my little cousin Leila from the country," said Meg to everyone they met. "Be nice to her. Find people to dance with her."

Strange faces smiled and strange voices answered, "Of course I will."

But Leila felt the girls didn't really see her. They were looking over at the men. Why didn't the men come over to ask the girls to dance? What were they waiting for? They just smiled and laughed and talked to each other.

But then at last they came, and the girls all smiled, excited. A tall, blond man came up to Meg and wrote something in her program. Meg passed him on to Leila.

"Could I have a dance?" he asked, and he wrote something in her program. Next came a dark man wearing glasses, then cousin Laurie with a friend, and Laura with a short man.

Lastly, an old, fat man with very little hair on his head came over. He took her program and looked at it. It was black with names now.

"Now let me see," he said. "Let me see . . ." He looked and looked at her program and then at his.

At last he wrote something and looked at her. "Do I remember you?" he asked softly. "Have we met before?"

Before Leila could answer, the music started up, and the fat man left. The music flew around the room, and people began to dance.

Leila watched for a moment, thinking of dancing lessons at school. Miss Eccles' loud voice in the smelly school hall. How very different from this beautiful room with this wonderful music! Oh, where was her first dance partner? She wanted to start dancing with someone soon. She must start dancing soon! Dance now or else fly right out of one of the dark windows!

"My dance, I think," someone said, smiling at her and holding out his arm.

Oh, good! She didn't need to fly away after all! The young man put his hand on her back, and then they danced away together like a flower in fast water.

"Pretty good floor[13], isn't it?" asked the young man in a quiet voice close to her ear.

"Oh, yes!" said Leila. "I think it's so nice and slippery[14]."

"Excuse me?" said the voice.

"It's so nice and slippery," said Leila again.

"Oh, yes," agreed the young man after a moment.

He danced so well. He was so strong, and he knew what he was doing. It was so nice to be dancing with a man and not one of the girls in Miss Eccles' class. Girls always stood on your feet or held you so hard it hurt.

"Were you at the Bell's ball last week?" came the young man's voice again.

"He sounds so tired," thought Leila. "Does he want to stop dancing?"

“No,” she answered. “This is my first dance.”

Her partner laughed. “No!” he said. He couldn’t believe it.

“Yes,” Leila said. “It really is the first dance I’ve been to.” It was so nice to tell somebody about it.

“You see, I’ve always lived in the country until now . . .”

At that moment the music stopped, and they went to sit on two chairs against the wall. Leila happily watched other men and women going out through the doors.

"Are you having a nice time, Leila?" asked Jose.

Then Laura passed and gave her a smile.

Her dance partner did not have much to say to her, but it wasn't important.

The music started up again and her second partner came over.

"The floor's not bad," he said.

"Do they always start by talking about the floor?" thought Leila.

And then, "Were you at the Neaves' on Tuesday?"

Leila told him it was her first ball. He didn't seem to be very interested – she didn't know why. Because it was so exciting! Her first ball! She was at the beginning of everything. Night wasn't just a dark, quiet, and beautifully sad thing anymore. It was full of light!

"Do you want an ice?" asked her partner. And they went out through the doors. Leila's face was hot, and she was very thirsty.

The ices looked so nice on little glass plates. And when they came back to the hall, there was the fat man waiting for her by the door.

Leila looked at him. He really *was* old. Why wasn't he sitting with the fathers and mothers?

"There you are," said the fat man. And he took her in his arms, and they began to dance very slowly. Leila thought it was more like walking than dancing.

"This is your first dance, isn't it?" he asked. Not one word about the floor!

"How did you know?" Leila asked.

"I know because I'm old," he said. "I know because of 30 years of coming to dances."

"Thirty years?" cried Leila. Twelve years before she was born!

"Terrible, isn't it?" agreed the fat man sadly.

Leila looked at him. She felt sorry for him. "I think it's wonderful that you're still coming to balls," she said kindly.

"That's very kind of you," the fat man said. He sang along softly to the music for a while, and then he said, "Of course, you won't be dancing like this for 30 years. Oh, no. Long before that you'll be sitting up there with the mothers and fathers in your nice black dress. Those pretty arms of yours will be short fat arms, and you'll smile like all those poor old women up there. You'll talk to the old lady next to you about *your* daughter."

Laura looked at him as he continued. "You'll say some man tried to kiss your daughter at the last ball. And your heart[15] will hurt because no one wants to kiss *you* now. And you'll say that these floors are so slippery and dangerous to walk on."

Leila gave a little laugh, but she did not feel like laughing. Was it true? It sounded true. At that moment, the music began to sound sad. Oh, how quickly things changed! Why didn't happiness last?

"I want to stop," she said in a small voice. The fat man led her to the door.

"No," she said, "I won't go outside. I won't sit down. I'll just stand here, thank you." She stood by the wall, trying to smile. But inside herself she felt like a sad little girl.

"Why did he have to say those terrible things?" she thought.

The fat man was looking at her. "You know, you mustn't worry about the things I say," he said.

"Oh, I won't," said Leila, holding her head up.

The music ended. Dancers walked past. The doors opened and closed. Leila didn't want to dance anymore. She wanted to be at home, sitting outside listening to those baby owls.

But then the music started again. It was beautiful music, and a young man came over to her. He smiled. Leila knew she had to dance with him until she could find Meg and tell her she wanted to go. Leila walked to the center of the floor. She didn't want to be there. She *didn't*.

But then the young man took her into his arms. They began to move around the room. And everything changed. It was like flying. The lights, the flowers, the dresses, and the pink faces, all became one beautiful flying wheel. It was wonderful!

Leila was smiling, smiling. And later, when she saw the fat man again, she smiled at him, too. She didn't even remember who he was.

ACTIVITIES PAGES 32–38

1 **Match the two parts of the sentences.**

1 Leila has never been to a ball [d]
2 The Sheridan girls aren't very excited about going to the ball [ ]
3 Leila wants to read the names of all the dances in the program [ ]
4 Leila didn't want to come to the ball [ ]
5 Leila doesn't answer the fat man's question [ ]

a because they always go to balls.
b because he leaves when the music starts.
c but there isn't any time.
~~d~~ because she lives in the country.
e but she isn't afraid anymore.

2 **Underline the correct words in each sentence.**

1 The Sheridan girls *know* / *don't know* it's Leila's first ball.
2 Leila wants to keep the *paper* / *gloves* so she can remember everything about the ball.
3 *Laura's* / *Leila's* special name is Twig.
4 The Sheridan girls and Leila go into the ladies' room *before* / *after* they go into the ballroom.
5 The girls and the men *are* / *aren't* on the same side of the room.
6 Meg *tells* / *doesn't tell* people in the ballroom that Leila is from the country.
7 Leila's first dance partner is *a young* / *an old fat* man.
8 The *young man* / *fat man* asks Leila about the floor.

ACTIVITIES PAGES 39–45

3 Are the sentences true (*T*) or false (*F*)?

1 Leila tells her first dance partner that she's never been to a ball. [T]
2 Leila and her first dance partner talk a lot after the music stops. [ ]
3 Leila's second dance partner asks her about the floor. [ ]
4 Leila doesn't tell her second dance partner that it's her first ball. [ ]
5 Leila dances again with her first partner. [ ]
6 The fat man doesn't know it's Leila's first ball. [ ]
7 The fat man says his first dance was 30 years ago. [ ]
8 Leila feels sad after dancing with the fat man. [ ]
9 After Leila dances with a young man she feels happy. [ ]

4 Answer the questions.

1 Who doesn't seem interested in Leila's first ball?

....

2 Who is waiting for Leila when she goes back inside the hall with her second dance partner?

....

3 Who doesn't ask Leila about the floor?

....

4 How does Leila feel at the end of the story?

....

The Doll's House

When old Mrs. Hay went back to town after staying with the Burnells, she sent the Burnell girls, Isabel, Lottie, and Kezia, a doll's house. It was very big, so Pat helped to carry it into the yard.

"It's summer," said Aunt Beryl. "It will be all right out there."

Aunt Beryl was worried about the strong smell of paint[16] that was coming from the doll's house.

"The smell could make someone sick," she thought. "Of course, it was very nice of Mrs. Hay to send it to the girls, but the smell really is awful! I hope the smell will go away before the doll's house needs to come into the house in the autumn."

So there was the doll's house out in the yard – a dark green color. The two chimneys on the roof were red and white, and the door was brown. There were four glass windows, and there was a small porch at the front of the house. The girls thought it was a beautiful house – beautiful! The smell wasn't important to them!

"Open it quickly, someone!" Isabel said.

Pat tried to open the house, but he couldn't. He had to get his knife and use it on the side of the house. But then all the front of the house opened, and you could see all the rooms: the living room and the dining room, the kitchen, and the two bedrooms. The girls loved seeing inside all the rooms at the same time.

“Oh . . . ,” they said, looking and looking. They were so happy with the house, they didn’t know what to say. It was just so wonderful. There was color on all the walls. And pictures. There was red carpet on all the floors, except the kitchen. There were red chairs in the living room, and green in the dining room. There were tables, beds, a stove for cooking food on, and even some small plates.

Kezia was the youngest of the girls. She liked the lamp best. She *really* liked the lamp. It was on the table in the dining room, and it was beautiful. The father and mother dolls were downstairs in the living room, and their two little children were asleep upstairs. The dolls were really too big for the doll’s house. They didn’t look right. But the lamp was right. To Kezia, the lamp was real, not a toy.

The Burnell girls hurried to school the next morning. They wanted to tell everybody about the doll's house before school started.

"I'll tell everyone," said Isabel. "Because I'm the oldest. Then you two can talk about it. But I'm telling everyone first." Lottie and Kezia didn't argue. There was nothing to say. Isabel *was* the oldest.

"I'm also going to choose who comes to see it first," Isabel continued importantly. "Mother said I could."

Mother said that while the doll's house was in the yard, the girls could ask some girls from school to come and see it.

"They can come two at a time," Mother told them, "Not to stay for tea or come into the house, but just to stand quietly in the yard and look at the doll's house."

The girls walked quickly, but it wasn't quick enough. When they got to school, class was about to start. There was only time to take their hats off and stand in line. Isabel looked very important and said behind her hand to the girls near her, "I've got something to tell you at playtime."

At playtime everyone wanted to be near Isabel. They all wanted to smile at her, to walk with her, or put their arms around her. Isabel felt very important. Everyone was waiting to hear what she had to say. The only girls who didn't go close were the little Kelveys. They knew Isabel and the other girls never wanted *them* to go near.

Mr. and Mrs. Burnell didn't really think the school was good enough for their girls, but it was the only school for miles. Everyone went there – the doctor's daughters, the shopkeeper's daughters, even the milkman's girls. But Mr. and Mrs. Burnell didn't want their daughters to speak to everybody. They certainly didn't want them to speak to the Kelveys. Isabel, Lottie, and Kezia walked past the Kelveys with their heads in the air. And because the Burnell girls did this, then so did everybody else. Even the teacher had a special voice for the Kelveys. When Lil Kelvey gave the teacher some flowers from the country, she said, "Thank you." But she smiled a special smile at everyone. The smile said, "Look at these poor flowers!"

The Kelveys were the daughters of the washerwoman who went from house to house every day, washing people's dirty clothes. This was bad enough. But where was Mr. Kelvey? Everyone said he was in prison[17]. The Kelveys were the daughters of a washerwoman and a man who was in prison! And they looked it. They wore things that people gave to Mrs. Kelvey – things they didn't want anymore.

For example, Lil Kelvey came to school in a dress made from the Burnells' old green tablecloth. She looked so funny! You had to laugh. Her little sister, Else, with her long white dress, looked like she was going to bed! *And* she wore boys' boots. But Else *did* make you smile with her short hair and her big eyes. She never spoke. She just went everywhere with Lil and held onto her sister's dress. That day at playtime, the Kelvey girls weren't standing as close to Isabel as the other girls. But they did listen. They didn't move when some of the girls turned to look at them in an unfriendly way.

Isabel's voice was loud as she told them all about the doll's house. She talked about the carpets, the beds, and the stove.

When she stopped talking, Kezia spoke up. "You forgot the lamp, Isabel," she said.

"Oh, yes," said Isabel, "There's a really small lamp on the

dining room table, all made of yellow and white glass. It looks real."

"The lamp's the best thing!" Kezia said. But nobody was listening. Isabel was choosing which two girls to invite back with them that afternoon to see the doll's house. She chose Emmie Cole and Lena Logan. But the other girls were still being very nice to Isabel. They wanted to see the doll's house another day. The Kelveys moved away.

Days passed. All the girls at school were talking about the doll's house. Everyone was saying, "Have you seen the Burnells' doll's house? Oh, isn't it beautiful?" They talked about it every lunchtime as they ate their sandwiches. And every lunchtime, the Kelvey girls listened. The Kelvey girls ate their sandwiches out of old newspaper. The other girls had meat in their sandwiches – the Kelveys had jam[18].

Kezia felt a little sorry for them.

"Mother," said Kezia one day, "can I ask the Kelveys to come and see thc house? Just once?"

Her mother looked at her. "No, Kezia!"

Kezia didn't understand why her mother was looking angry. "But why not?" she said. "They're the only girls from school who haven't come."

"Go away, Kezia," said her mother. "You know why they can't come."

The weeks passed, and now the girls at school didn't talk about the doll's house so often at lunchtime. The doll's house wasn't new to them now. But they didn't really know what else to talk about. One day they looked at the Kelveys, eating their sandwiches out of newspaper. They were always alone – just the two sisters – no one else. And they were always listening. The girls wanted to be unkind to them.

Emmie Cole started it. "Lil Kelvey's going to be a servant when she leaves school," she said.

"Ooh, how awful!" said Isabel Burnell, and she looked at Emmie.

"It's true, it's true," said Emmie.

"I'll go and ask her," said Lena Logan.

"You can't!" said Jessie May.

"I'm not afraid!" said Lena. "Watch! Watch me! Watch me now!" And she went over to the Kelveys.

Lil looked up from her lunch. Else stopped eating. What was coming now?

"You're going to be a servant when you leave school, aren't you, Lil Kelvey?" asked Lena in a high voice.

Lil didn't answer. She just smiled. The girls who were watching began to laugh.

Lena was angry. She put her face close to Lil's. "Your father's in prison!" she said unkindly.

The girls couldn't believe what Lena was saying. It was a really bad thing to say! But it was exciting, too, and they all ran away to play, shouting and laughing.

In the afternoon, Pat came for the Burnell girls, and they drove home. There were visitors. Isabel and Lottie liked visitors, and they went upstairs to change their clothes. But Kezia went quietly out of the back door into the yard. Looking out along the road, she saw two small children. As they got nearer, she saw they were the Kelveys – Lil in front and Else close behind.

Kezia started to run away. Then she stopped. The Kelveys came nearer. Kezia decided to speak to them.

"Hello," she said.

The Kelveys stopped. They couldn't believe Kezia was speaking to them. Lil smiled. Else just looked.

"You can come and see our doll's house if you want to," said Kezia.

But Lil's face turned red. "Oh, no," she said.

"Why not?" asked Kezia.

Lil's face was still red. "You can't speak to us," she said. "Your mother doesn't want you to. Our mother told us."

"Oh, well," said Kezia. "You can come anyway. No one's looking."

"No," said Lil.

"Don't you want to?" asked Kezia.

Else pulled on Lil's skirt. Lil turned to look at her sister. Else's eyes were very big. She really wanted to go. When Else pulled her skirt again, Lil started to walk. Kezia went in front, and the two Kelvey girls came behind her like two little lost cats.

"There it is," said Kezia when they got to the doll's house.

Lil and Else looked and looked.

"I'll open it for you," Kezia said kindly.

She opened it. "There's the living room and the dining room, and that's the –"

"Kezia! Kezia!" It was Aunt Beryl's voice.

All three girls turned around. Aunt Beryl was standing at the back door. She looked very angry.

"Kezia!" she said again. "Why are the little Kelveys in the yard? You know your mother doesn't allow you to talk to them! Run away, children. Run away! And don't come back again!"

The Kelvey girls hurried away across the yard and through the white gate.

"You bad girl!" Aunt Beryl shouted angrily at Kezia, and she closed the front of the doll's house loudly. Aunt Beryl wasn't having a good afternoon. Everything was going wrong, and now this.

"I feel better now that I've shouted at Kezia and those little Kelveys," she thought, and she went back into the house singing softly.

When the Kelveys were a long way from the Burnells' house, they sat down to rest by the side of the road. Lil's face was still hot. She took off her hat. The two girls sat and looked out over the grass at the cows by the river.

Else moved closer to her sister. She wasn't thinking about the cows, or the angry woman. She smiled.

"I saw the little lamp," she said softly.

Then they were both quiet again.

ACTIVITIES PAGES 48–53

1 Match the two parts of the sentences.

1 Aunt Beryl puts the doll's house in the yard [c]
2 The Burnell girls think that the doll's house [ ]
3 Kezia really likes [ ]
4 Nobody speaks to the Kelvey girls at school [ ]
5 At school, the Kelvey girls wear [ ]
6 All the girls stand close to Isabel and listen to the story except for [ ]

a clothes that other people give them.
b because they're poor.
c because she doesn't like the smell.
d the Kelvey girls.
e the lamp.
f is beautiful.

2 Underline the correct words in each sentence.

1 The doll's house is *in the yard / inside the house.*
2 *Lottie and Kezia / Isabel* will tell everybody first at school about the doll's house.
3 *Isabel / Mrs. Burnell* is going to choose who comes to see the doll's house first.
4 Mr. and Mrs. Burnell *like / don't like* the school.
5 The school has *only rich / rich and poor* girls.
6 Mr. and Mrs. Burnell *want / don't want* their daughters to speak to the Kelvey girls.
7 The Kelvey girls' mother *is a washerwoman / is in prison.*
8 Isabel forgets to talk about *the lamp / the carpets, the beds, and the stove.*

ACTIVITIES PAGES 54–59

3 **Complete the sentences with the names in the box.**

Kezia	The Kelvey girls (x3)	Else	One of the girls

1 ....The Kelvey girls.... have jam sandwiches at lunchtime.

2 .... are the only girls from school who haven't come to see the doll's house.

3 .... says terrible things to the Kelveys at lunchtime.

4 .... speaks to the Kelvey girls.

5 .... wants to see the doll's house.

6 .... run from the Burnell yard.

4 **Answer the questions.**

1 Why does Kezia feel sorry for the Kelvey girls at lunchtime?

....

2 Why doesn't Mrs. Burnell want the Kelvey girls to come and see the house?

....

3 List two things Lena tells Lil Kelvey.

....

4 Who tells the Kelvey girls to leave the yard?

....

LOOKING BACK

5 **Check your answers to *Before you read* on page 3.**

Glossary

[1]**marquee** (page 4) *noun* a large tent used for parties that happen outside

[2]**class** (page 8) *noun* a group of people who have the same way of life or social and economic background

[3]**hall** (page 9) *noun* the room just inside the front door of a house, which goes into other rooms

[4]**carpet** (page 11) *noun* a material used on floors of buildings

[5]**weary** (page 11) *adjective* tired

[6]**cottage** (page 15) *noun* a small house, usually in the country

[7]**silly** (page 15) *adjective* stupid

[8]**gate** (page 15) *noun* a door in a fence or outside wall

[9]**waiter** (page 19) *noun* a man who brings food and drink to people

[10]**glove** (page 33) *noun* a piece of clothing that you put over your fingers and hand

[11]**silver** (page 35) *adjective* a gray and white color

[12]**owl** (page 35) noun a type of bird with large eyes

[13]**floor** (page 38) *noun* an area where something happens, such as a dance floor

[14]**slippery** (page 38) *adjective* if something is slippery, it is difficult to walk on

[15]**heart** (page 43) *noun* the thing inside your chest that sends blood around your body

[16]**paint** (page 48) *noun* a colored liquid that you put on a wall or a thing

[17]**prison** (page 52) *noun* a place where people go because they did something very bad

[18]**jam** (page 54) *noun* a sweet food made from fruit that you put on bread; for example, strawberry jam